W9-CCD-063

First published in Great Britain 2016 by Red Shed,
an imprint of Egmont UK Limited
The Yellow Building, 1 Nicholas Road,
London W11 4AN

www.egmont.co.uk

Text copyright © Jess French 2016
Illustrations copyright © Jonathan Woodward 2016
Paper engineering copyright © Keith Finch 2016
The moral rights of the author, illustrator and
paper engineer have been asserted.

ISBN 978 1 4052 7756 3

A CIP catalogue record for this book is available
from the British Library.
No part of this publication may be reproduced, stored in
a retrieval system, or transmitted, in any form or by any
means, electronic, mechanical, photocopying, recording
or otherwise, without the prior permission of the publisher
and copyright owner.

MIX
Paper from
responsible sources
FSC® C018306

The publisher would like to thank the following for permission to reproduce
their material. Every care has been taken to trace copyright holders. However,
if there have been unintentional omissions or failure to trace copyright holders,
we apologize and will, if informed, endeavour to make corrections in any
future edition.

(OFC = Outside Front Cover, OBC = Outside Back Cover, b = bottom,
c = centre, l = left, r = right, t = top)

OFC, OBC, 4–5, 6, 23tr (stick) andersphoto/Shutterstock; OFC, 4–5 (leaf)
reiza/Shutterstock; OBCtl, 4 Kindle Entertainment Productions Ltd;
7tr, 20–21c, 21tr (stone) Nik Merkulov/Shutterstock; 7tr, 21r (leaf) Nik
Merkulov/Shutterstock; 7c Brian A Jackson/Shutterstock; 7tr, 7bl, 20l Torsak
Thammachote/Shutterstock; 8r Alexey Tarasenko/Shutterstock; 8l (bookcase)
mmphotographie.de/Shutterstock; 9 Eugene Sergeev/Shutterstock;
10bl, 10–11c, 12 (leaf) Labrador Photo Video/Shutterstock; 11r Nomad_Soul/
Shutterstock; 10–11 (sky) mexrix/Shutterstock; 13 Maksimilian/Shutterstock;
14, 15 Maja H./Shutterstock; 16 Madlen/Shutterstock; 17 (box) Everything/
Shutterstock; 17 (log) farres/Shutterstock; 17 (cardboard roll) V. J. Matthew/
Shutterstock; 17 (leaves) asawinimages/Shutterstock; 18–19 K. Miri
Photography/Shutterstock; 22 dek-dokkhamtai/Shutterstock; 23cr weedezign/
Shutterstock; 24tc MarkMirror/Shutterstock; 24tr Bill Frische/Shutterstock;
24br Matteo photos/Shutterstock; 24bc Dr. Morley Read/Shutterstock;
24tl, 25bl AppStock/Shutterstock; 25tc Liew Weng Keong/Shutterstock;
25tr D. Kucharski K. Kucharska/Shutterstock; 25bc Dutourdumonde
Photography/Shutterstock; 25tl dirkr/Shutterstock; 25br jovengandalf/Creative
Commons Attribution–Share Alike 2.0 Generic Licence/http://bit.ly/1TK8QxG;
26tc Mike Thorsen; 26tr Nigel Catlin/Visuals Unlimited/Corbis; 26br Imfoto/
Shutterstock; 26bc Ryan M. Bolton/Shutterstock; 26bl greksa/Shutterstock;
26tl Mauro Rodrigues/Shutterstock; 27tc kurt_G/Shutterstock; 27tr Dant
Fenolio/Science Photo Library; 27br Paul E Marek/Creative Commons
Attribution 3.0 Unported Licence/http://bit.ly/1lf0eq6; 27bl Bo Valentino/
Shutterstock; 27tl Chatchai Somwat/Shutterstock; 28 Horiyan/Shutterstock;
29 Pavol Kmeto/Shutterstock.
Stay safe online. Any website addresses listed in this book are
correct at the time of going to print. However, Egmont is not
responsible for content hosted by third parties. Please be
aware that online content can be subject to change
and websites can contain content that is unsuitable
for children. We advise that all children are
supervised when using the internet.

Join Jess on a minibeast adventure!

Tickly
Minibeast
Adventures

with Jess French

RED SHED

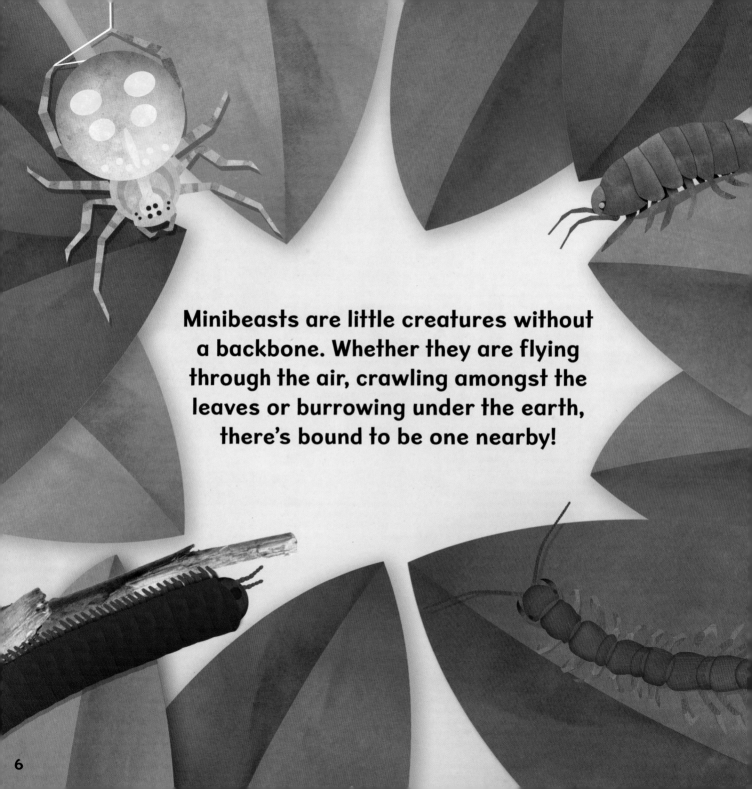

Minibeasts are little creatures without a backbone. Whether they are flying through the air, crawling amongst the leaves or burrowing under the earth, there's bound to be one nearby!

A magnifying glass or bug box can help us get a closer look at minibeasts.

The magnifying glass makes the minibeast look bigger.

magnifying glass

We might want to use one to look at some of the creatures in this book.

Today we're going out exploring in search of tickly minibeasts. Let's go!

7

Tickly minibeasts are everywhere! Some of them even live in our houses. Let's see if we can find some spiders first.

You might find one behind a plant.

There might be one hiding in a corner.

They like to hide in dark, quiet places.

Spiders are scared of people, so they might run away if we get too close!

This spider is stuck in the sink because it cannot climb the slippery sides!

We can help spiders escape from a sink or bath by hanging a towel over the edge.

Spiders have:

bodies made of
two parts

up to
eight eyes

eight legs

Minibeasts with eight legs
are called arachnids.

9

Many spiders spin webs to trap their food. Look – this one has caught a fly!

The web is made of silk, a special string that the spider pulls out of its bottom!

Spiders' webs are shiny, strong and very beautiful.

When minibeasts land on the spider's sticky web, they cannot wriggle free.

fly

egg sac

Mummy spiders wrap their
eggs in silk to keep them safe.

Some spiders use their silk
to swing through the air
and escape danger.

A few types of spider
hide inside tunnels
made of their own silk!

**Spiders are not the only minibeasts with
eight legs. Shall we go and find some more?**

Can you see the minibeast hiding in this bush? It looks like a spider on stilts, but it is not. It is called a harvestman.

Harvestmen have:

bodies made of one part

two eyes

eight long, thin legs

Harvestmen don't make webs to trap their food. They eat whatever they can find lying around, such as dead minibeasts, plants or poo!

bird

Some people call
the harvestman
a daddy-long-legs!

leg

If a harvestman thinks it is going to be eaten, it can drop off one of its legs!

This surprises the attacker, and gives the harvestman time to run away.

Some creatures have EVEN MORE legs than spiders and harvestmen! Shall we see if we can find them?

13

Here's one under this leaf! It is a woodlouse. Under here it is nice and dark, just how woodlice like it.

Its legs might be short, but it can still run very fast!

Shall we count how many legs a woodlouse has?

1 2 3 4 5 6 7 8 9 10 11 12 13 14

It has 14 short legs.

The woodlouse has a hard shell to keep its soft body safe.

hard shell

antennae (feelers)

If they are scared, some woodlice have an amazing trick to give them extra protection . . .

They can roll into a ball!

As the woodlouse gets bigger, it grows a new shell underneath the old one. Then the old shell falls off!

Woodlice are very friendly and live in big groups, so there must be some more nearby. Let's take a look . . .

Wow! We have found a whole woodlouse family!

However much a woodlouse drinks, it never needs to wee. Instead its shell lets out a smelly gas!

Woodlouse mummies usually have about 25 babies at once! They cling on to their mummy's tummy.

The mummy woodlouse will take care of her babies until they are big enough to look after themselves.

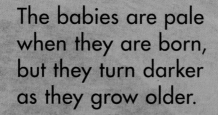

The babies are pale when they are born, but they turn darker as they grow older.

woodlouse baby

Shall we make a woodlouse hotel? Then we can get a closer look at these minibeasts.

1. First, turn a box on its side.

2. Then make the bottom layer with something woodlice find yummy, such as dead leaves.

3. Now put rolled-up cardboard or bits of wood on top for woodlice to hide under.

4. Woodlice like damp places, so sprinkle the inside of the hotel with water using a bottle or watering can.

Other minibeasts like dark, damp places, too. Maybe we can find some under this rock . . .

Look! Under the rock are two different types of minibeast — centipedes and millipedes.

They are both long and wriggly with lots of legs. We can use a magnifying glass to take a closer look.

So how can we tell the difference betwee

Centipedes have:
14 to over 300 legs
flat bodies
long antennae

They run very fast!

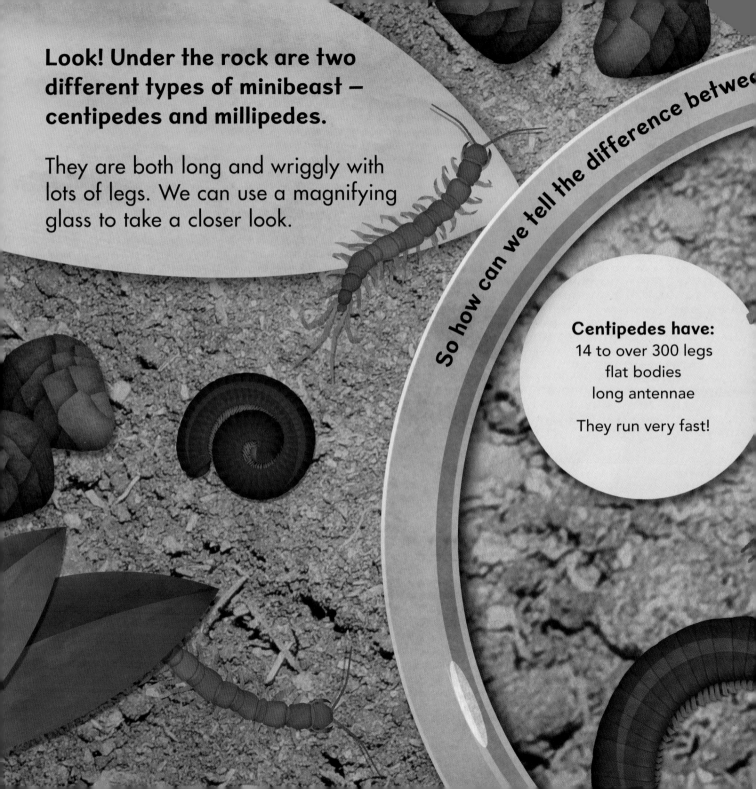

entipedes and millipedes?

Centipedes and millipedes do not breathe through their mouths like us. Instead they use tiny holes in the sides of their bodies!

Millipedes have:
40 to 750 legs
round bodies
short antennae

They crawl along slowly.

Let's have a closer look at this centipede's legs. Do you think it ever trips over?

The legs at the back of its body are longer than the ones at the front. This means the centipede NEVER trips over!

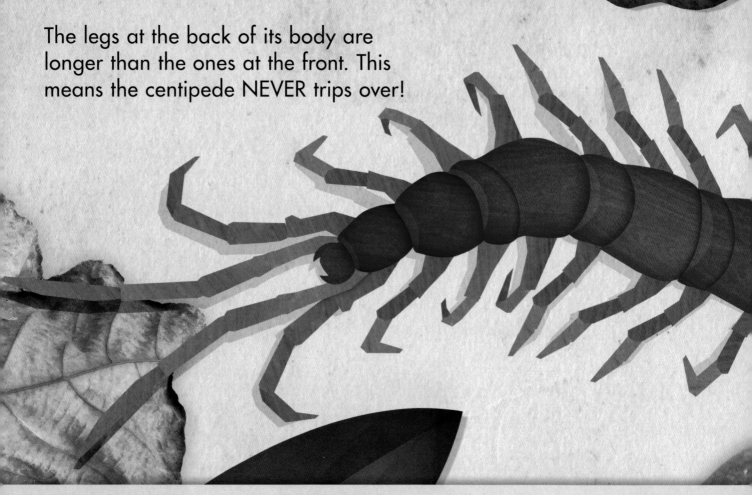

Let's make a fingerprint centipede.

1. Dip your fingers in paint and press them on to a piece of paper to create the sections of your centipede's body.

2. Use a pen or pencil to draw the legs, antennae, claws and eyes.

3. Centipedes have two legs on each section of their bodies, one on each side.

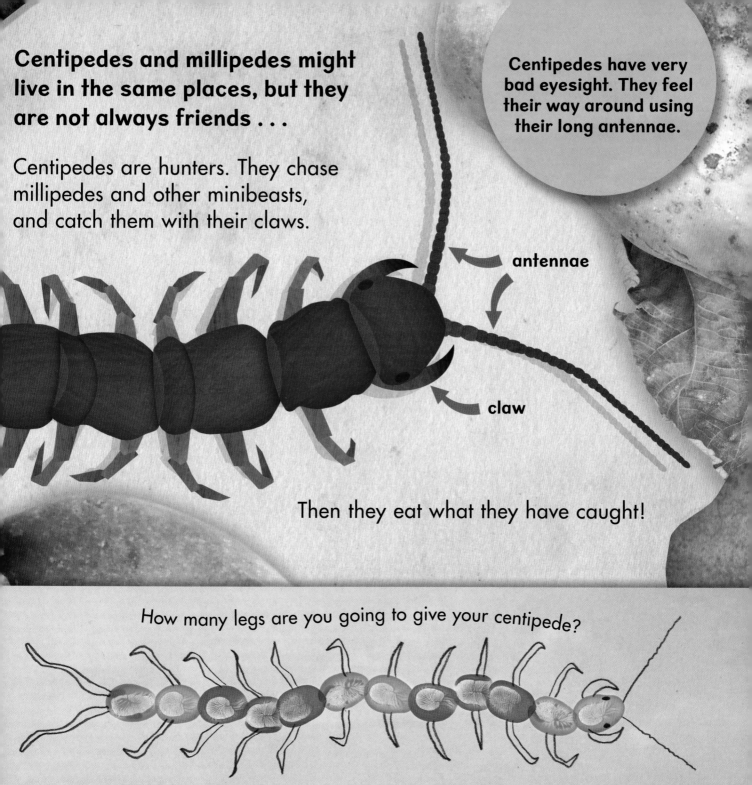

Centipedes and millipedes might live in the same places, but they are not always friends . . .

Centipedes are hunters. They chase millipedes and other minibeasts, and catch them with their claws.

Centipedes have very bad eyesight. They feel their way around using their long antennae.

antennae

claw

Then they eat what they have caught!

How many legs are you going to give your centipede?

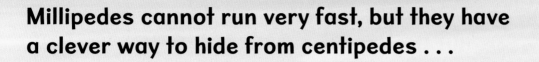

Millipedes cannot run very fast, but they have a clever way to hide from centipedes . . .

They can dig deep into the soil to escape danger.

Millipedes have more legs than any other animal in the world!

Down here they can find dead plants and wood to eat.

A millipede's legs are so strong that it can climb trees and even hang upside down!

poo

They poo out new soil that is full of nutrients and perfect for new plants to grow in.

What a brilliant day of minibeast hunting! Get ready to find some more on our next adventure!

Mexican red knee tarantula
These hairy spiders are popular pets.

Funnel weaver spider
They live inside a funnel-shaped web.

Spiny orb weaver
They have huge spikes on their bodies!

Jess's favourite **tickly** minibeasts

Brazilian wandering spider
These are the world's most venomous spiders.

Black widow spider
Females will bite anything that comes near their egg sac!

Golden wheel spider

When in danger, they fold up their legs and roll away like a wheel!

Jumping spider

They can jump ten to 50 times their own body length!

Diving bell spider

They breathe underwater by spinning a web like a bubble and filling it with air.

Goliath bird-eating spider

They are some of the world's heaviest spiders – and they can eat birds!

Golden orb weaver

These spiders spin the biggest webs.

Goliath harvestman

Unlike most harvestmen, these are predators and eat live worms!

Pill woodlouse
These woodlice can roll up into a ball.

Spiky yellow woodlouse
These are some of the rarest woodlice in the world.

Rosy woodlouse
They are a pink-orange colour with a yellow stripe down their middle.

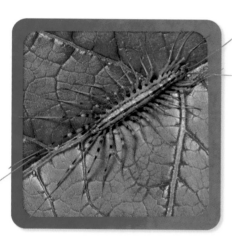

House centipede
They have longer legs than any other centipede.

Peruvian giant yellow centipede
These are the world's biggest centipedes. They can grow up to 30 centimetres long!

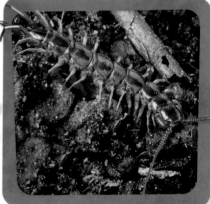

Common centipede
These centipedes are the most widespread throughout the world.

Shocking pink dragon millipede
They ooze poison from their spiny bodies!

Pill millipede
They can roll into a ball – a bit like a pill woodlouse.

Sierra luminous millipede
These special millipedes glow in the dark.

Giant African millipede
The biggest millipedes in the world can grow up to 37 centimetres long.

Illacme plenipes
These are the millipedes with the most legs – up to 750. They only have a scientific name because we haven't known about them for long. They were first seen in 1926, but not spotted again until 2005!

Glossary

antennae
Feelers on the heads of many minibeasts. They use them to smell and find their way around.

arachnids
Creatures with eight legs but no antennae or wings, such as spiders and harvestmen.

backbone
A line of bones running down an animal's body. Minibeasts don't have a backbone.

egg sac
A case that spiders spin to keep their eggs safe.

minibeast
A small animal with no backbone, such as a butterfly, worm or spider.

nutrients
Parts of food that animals and plants need to survive and grow.

silk
Strong thread made by spiders.

Index

antennae 15, 18, 19, 21
arachnids 9

babies 16, 17
backbones 6
bodies 9, 12, 15, 18, 19

centipedes 18–21, 26
claws 21

daddy-long-legs 13

eggs 11, 24
eyes 9, 12, 21

harvestmen 12–13, 25

leaves 6, 14, 17
legs 9, 12, 13, 14, 18–19, 20, 22–23, 26, 27

magnifying glasses 7, 18
millipedes 18–19, 21, 22–23, 27

nutrients 23

plants 12, 22, 23
poo 12, 23

shells 15, 16
silk 10–11
soil 17, 22, 23
spiders 8–11, 24–25

webs 10, 24, 25
wood 17, 22
woodlice 14–17, 26